HUMANS IN SPACE

EXPLORING PLANET MARS

DAVID JEFFERIS AND MAT IRVINE

Crabtree Publishing Company

www.crabtreebooks.com

Introduction

Welcome to the world of human space flight, and to the "red planet" Mars, future target for space explorers. When will we be ready for the first human flight to Mars? There is no exact date set for the first flight, and many years of effort will go into developing the equipment to make an expedition possible. If all goes well, the first Mars ship could leave the Earth on a long and dangerous journey around 2025 . . .

Crabtree Publishing Company
PMB 16A,
350 Fifth Avenue, Suite 3308,
New York, NY 10118

616 Welland Avenue,
St. Catharines,
Ontario L2M 5V6

Coordinating Editor: Ellen Rodger
Editors:
Carrie Gleason, Adrianna Morganelli,
Jennifer Lackey
Production Coordinator: Rose Gowsell
Prepress technician: Nancy Johnson

© 2007 Crabtree Publishing Company

Educational Advisor: Julie Stapleton
Text Editor: Isabella McIntyre
Written and produced by:
David Jefferis and Mat Irvine/Buzz Books

©2007 David Jefferis/Buzz Books

Library of Congress
Cataloging-in-Publication Data

Jefferis, David.
  Exploring Planet Mars / written by David Jefferis & Mat Irvine.
     p. cm. -- (Humans in space)
  Includes index.
  ISBN-13: 978-0-7787-3100-9 (rlb)
  ISBN-10: 0-7787-3100-6 (rlb)
  ISBN-13: 978-0-7787-3114-6 (pb)
  ISBN-10: 0-7787-3114-6 (pb)
  1. Mars (Planet)--Juvenile literature. 2. Mars (Planet)--Exploration--Juvenile literature.
  I. Irvine, Mat. II. Title. III. Series.

QB641.J44 2007
523.43--dc22

2007003461

Pictures from right, clockwise:
1   A scientist in the future inspects a Martian rock, using a hammer.
2   The Earth, Moon, and Mars, shown to the same scale.
3   Setting up a base.
4   Taking samples.
5   A future Mars ship crew salutes for the camera.
6   The plains and valleys of Mars.

Contents

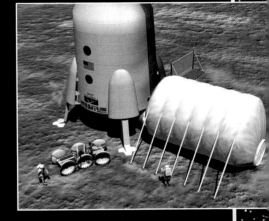

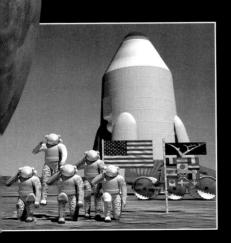

Circling the Sun

▲ Mars was the Roman god of war, symbolized by a circle with an arrowhead. These represent a warrior's shield and spear.

Earth and Mars are two of the eight major **planets** that move around the Sun. Together, the Sun, planets, and other small objects form the **Solar System**.

Each planet moves around the Sun in a huge path called an **orbit**. The time it takes a planet to complete a single orbit is called a **year**. The length of a planet's year depends on its distance from the Sun and the speed at which it travels through space. Earth orbits the Sun every 365 days, but Mars is farther from the Sun, so its year is 687 Earth-days, nearly twice as long.

Planning a mission to Mars is a challenge greater than any space flight that has yet been attempted. The most distant place that humans have ever reached is the Moon, visited by astronauts of the U.S. Apollo program. It took them about three days to fly from Earth to the Moon, a distance of some 239,000 miles (384,000 kilometers).

The red planet is much farther away. Even when Earth and Mars are at their closest, they are still 35 million miles (56 million kilometers) apart.

8

◄ Here are the major planets that circle the Sun. They are shown to the same scale for size, but the vast distances between them are far greater than can be pictured accurately here.

As well as the planets shown here, there are also many **dwarf planets**, such as Pluto and Eris, and millions of other chunks of rock and ice.
1   Mercury
2   Venus
3   Earth (marked in yellow)
4   Mars (marked in yellow)
5   Jupiter
6   Saturn
7   Uranus
8   Neptune
The four inner planets are all rocky worlds, but only Earth has oceans and breathable air. The huge outer planets are made up mostly of vast amounts of gases.

8

MARSFACT
Mars is a smaller planet than the Earth – it is only about half as wide, with just one-quarter of Earth's surface area. But since the red planet has no rivers, seas, or oceans, its land area is only a little less than that of the much bigger Earth.

The great "canal" debate

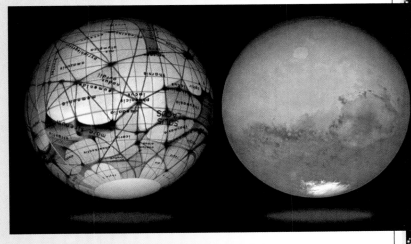

▲ An early map of Mars (left), compared with a spaceprobe image

For a long time people have wondered if there is life on Mars. In 1877, Italian astronomer Giovanni Schiaparelli thought he saw many straight lines on the surface through his telescope. He called the lines *canali*, which means "channels" in Italian. Over time, the word was mistranslated and channels became "canals" in English-speaking countries. In the United States, leading astronomer Percival Lowell thought that the canals might be signs of an ancient Martian civilization trying to survive on a dying, desert world. Lowell suggested that the canals were built by the Martians to carry water from icy regions at the North and South poles of Mars, to irrigate the deserts. Many experts disagreed with Lowell, such as astronomer Eugène Antoniadi, who worked in France. At first Antoniadi had found Lowell's ideas exciting, but when he studied Mars in 1909, he found no signs of any canals. Even so, many scientists remained hopeful of life on Mars until 1964, when the space probe Mariner 4 showed a world with craters and deserts, but no signs of life.

Percival Lowell

Astronomer Eugène Antoniadi

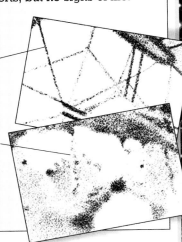

Schiaparelli's sketch shows lines. He called them *canali*

Antoniadi's later drawing showed no lines at all

Looking at Mars

Before today's high-tech instruments became available, astronomers could only peer through Earth-based telescopes and make sketches of their observations.

▲ The first space probe to land on Mars was Viking 1, in 1976. It tested the soil for any signs of life.

From Earth, Mars appears as little more than a bright red star. This is not too surprising, considering that it is a small planet a great distance away. It was not until space probes visited the planet in the 1960s and 1970s that we could see the surface in some detail.

▲ This picture of Mars was taken by the **Hubble Space Telescope**. It is about the best view of Mars available from close to Earth.

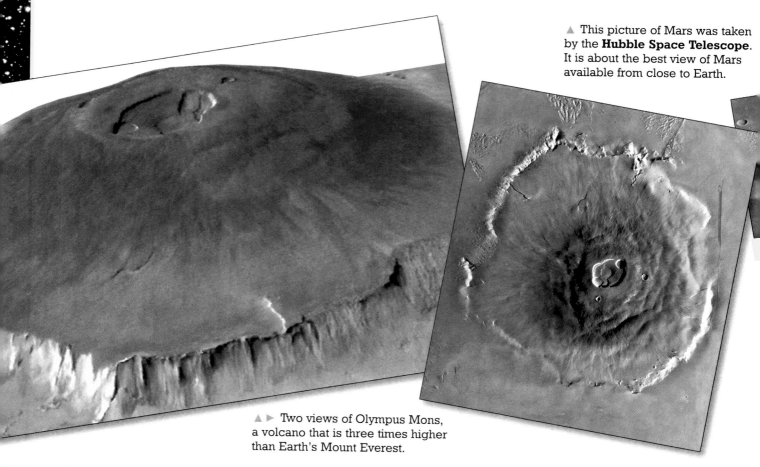

▲ ▶ Two views of Olympus Mons, a volcano that is three times higher than Earth's Mount Everest.

Earth and Mars compared

Earth and Mars are both rocky planets, but Earth is larger, measuring about 7,927 miles (12,756 kilometers) across. Mars is just 4,220 miles (6,794 kilometers) across. The length of a day on each planet is similar. A Martian day, at 24 hours and 37.5 minutes, is only a little longer than Earth's 24-hour day. A Martian day is called a "**sol**."

Mars is mostly desert, with an **atmosphere** far too thin to breathe. Scientists believe Mars may have had shallow seas once, but today any water is thought to be below ground or frozen into ice at the poles.

Even in high summer, noon on Mars is only as warm as a spring day on Earth. The nights are bitterly cold, with temperatures always dropping far below freezing.

Earth's **Moon** has a surface area about the same size as Africa, but the two moons of Mars, Phobos and Deimos, are potato-shaped lumps of rock only a few miles across. Despite all these differences, Mars is the most Earth-like of all the planets!

Earth · Moon · Mars · Phobos · Deimos

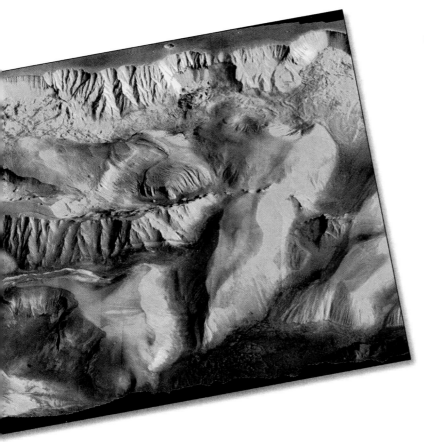

Today much of Mars has been photographed in detail from space, but **landers** are still needed to show what it is actually like on the ground. By 2007, robotic vehicles had driven over only a small area of the planet, so there is plenty of Mars left to discover.

The top targets for future exploration of Mars, both by robots and by humans, are Olympus Mons and Valles Marineris. Mars' Olympus Mons is the biggest volcano in the Solar System, and Valles Marineris is the deepest and longest **rift valley**.

◀ A view of Valles Marineris, showing just a few of its many huge, winding canyons.

▼ Mars also has vast flat deserts, as seen in this picture taken by a Mars **rover** named *Spirit* in 2003.

MARSFACT
Mars is also known as the "red planet." Its surface is a reddish-brown color because much of it is covered with rust. The rust is caused by the iron-rich soil reacting chemically with the tiny amount of oxygen in Mars' atmosphere.

Life on Mars?

The idea of alien creatures on Mars is an exciting one, but the Martians of sci-fi stories do not seem to exist.

▲ The Mars rock is called ALH 84001, a label that marks the place where it was found.

► These tiny objects, here colored blue, were thought at first to be tiny forms of life from Mars.

In 1984, a lump of rock was found lying on the ice of **Antarctica**. Millions of years ago, the rock was blown across space by a huge explosion on Mars. Scientists inspected the rock using microscopes – and thought they saw remains of Martian life!

The War of the Worlds

Percival Lowell's canal ideas caused a worldwide wave of interest in the possibility of life on other worlds.

In 1898, *The War of the Worlds* was published. It was a sci-fi novel by British author H.G. Wells, and an amazing tale that described a deadly invasion from another world. Tall, three-legged Martian war machines stalked across our world, destroying anything that tried to stop them.

Not only that, but Wells also imagined his Martians as **alien** vampire creatures that lived off the blood of their human victims.

In 1938, a radio play of Wells' story was broadcast in the form of a "real" news item. It was so convincing that thousands of people, listening to the play on their radios, thought that an invasion was really happening.

A musical has been made of the story, as have several movies.

British author H.G. Wells

Early illustration shows a Martian war machine firing a deadly heat ray

▲ American author Edgar Rice Burroughs' novels about Mars featured a planet full of alien life, from beautiful princesses to dangerous monsters.

◀ The Phoenix lander is planned as a robotic biological laboratory. This means that it will have tools that may be able to tell us if there is life when it lands on Mars' polar regions in 2010.

In 1996, scientists studying the Mars rock announced that there was "Life on Mars." The "life" was just a few rod-like structures, visible only through a microscope. After further analysis, many other scientists decided that the rods were not life forms, but the result of chemical reactions in the rock. Another Mars rock, called Nakhla, shows similar structures. The only real agreement between scientists is that more Mars exploration needs to be done.

MARSFACT
The ice caps of Mars are weird places. At the south pole, jets of carbon dioxide gas erupt from under the ice. Near the pole, huge geysers of gas and dust blow high into the air.

Wells described his Martians as octopus-like creatures, about the size of a small bear

Steven Spielberg's 2005 movie remake showed war machines looking much like Wells' originals

In the 1953 *War of the Worlds* movie, the war machines could fly. Each machine was protected by an invisible energy shield

Building a Mars ship

Designing and building a crewed Mars spacecraft has never been done before, so it will be a challenging job.

Creating a spacecraft that will carry humans to Mars is a long way from detailed planning, but ideas are taking shape. The giant space liners of sci-fi movies are not possible because the cost and technical challenges of building them are far too great.

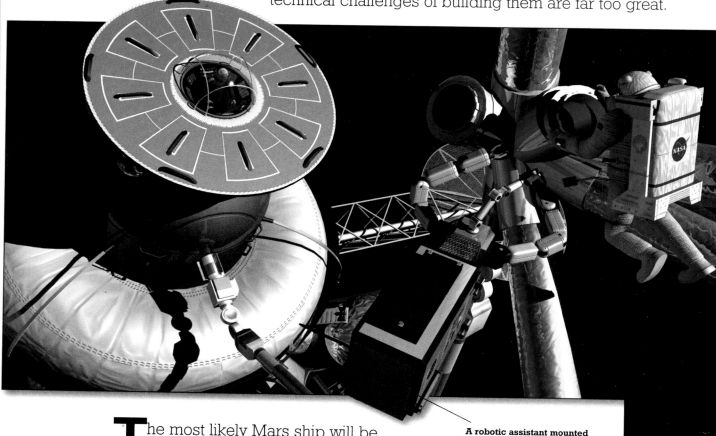

The most likely Mars ship will be similar to today's spacecraft. It will have fuel tanks placed ahead of rocket engines. At the front will be the living, storage, and command **modules**.

The sections of a Mars spacecraft will be built as separate modules, and equipped with wiring, electronics, and other equipment on Earth. Then the modules will be taken into Earth orbit, and assembled in space.

A robotic assistant mounted on a long moveable arm

▲ An illustration showing a future astronaut floating in space while helping with assembly. A robotic assistant is guided by a second astronaut inside the crew module's transparent viewer.

► This design for a Mars ship has an inflatable crew cabin. A test version was flown in 2006.

The engines will probably burn a **liquid fuel**, such as the mixture of **hydrogen** and oxygen used by the main engines of the U.S. Space Shuttle.

Alternative energy sources include a **nuclear motor**, similar to a system developed in the 1960s. This system uses heated gases to provide thrust, or the force that pushes the spacecraft forward. Systems like this give far more power than chemical fuels.

Many people are concerned about the safety of using nuclear energy, because of the danger to the environment if there was an explosion during launch from Earth.

How do nuclear motors work?

Traditional rocket engines burn a fuel, such as liquid hydrogen, by mixing it with liquid oxygen. The resulting flame and hot gases roar out of the nozzle to give thrust.

A nuclear engine also uses a fuel, but turns it into a gas by heating it with the high energy of atoms in a shielded container. The result is a huge amount of thrust. An early motor was built in the 1960s, but the project was cancelled before it could be used on a spacecraft.

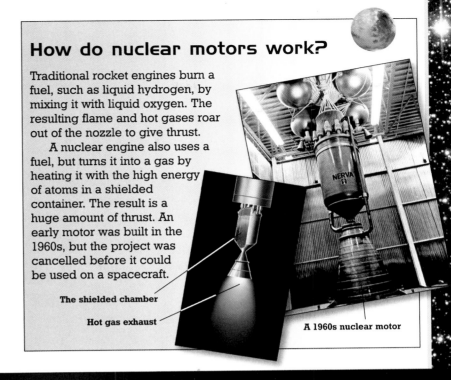

The shielded chamber

Hot gas exhaust

A 1960s nuclear motor

MARSFACT
All sorts of debris drifts through space, such as dust and rocks, even the remains of old **comets**. A Mars ship will need to have a double-hull shield for protection against a collision, much like those built in ocean liners in case of hitting an iceberg.

COUNTDOWN TO MARS

If all goes well, the first mission to Mars could take place on this schedule:

2010 Development of equipment continues.
2015 Planning of mission complete.
2020 Construction of Mars spacecraft begins.
2025 First expedition leaves for Mars.
2027 Mars crew returns to Earth.

Training the Marsnauts

Testing lightweight Mars suits has already begun. Here are two designs, being worn to see if they work properly.

Anyone flying on a space mission needs an immense amount of training. Marsnauts, or astronauts who visit Mars, will need to learn many extra skills.

The basics of a space flight career are much the same, whatever the mission. First, the astronauts have to be very dedicated, as it takes many years of work and study before they are ready for a space flight. They also need university training in engineering, biology, or another science. It helps if they are pilots – and of course, they need to be healthy. Space is big, but spacecraft are not, so they need to get along well with other people in confined spaces. Missions to Mars will be long, so being calm and patient will also be very important.

◄ Nowhere on Earth matches the Martian terrain exactly. Desert regions are the closest, and it is here that Marsnauts could carry out some of their training. The suits shown here are real, as are the backpacks, which contain an air supply and radio.

MARSFACT
Space suits for Mars may look similar to the suits used today, but they will need to be lighter in weight. Suits used for space walks in Earth orbit would weigh more than 106 pounds (48 kg) on Mars, heavy enough to exhaust a wearer in a short time.

"Doctor, I don't feel very well..."

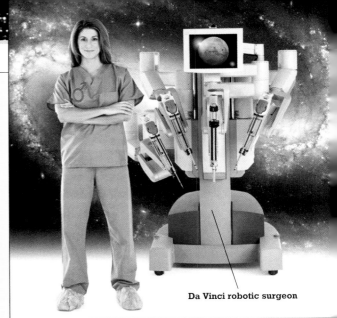

Da Vinci robotic surgeon

What will happen if one of the Marsnauts gets seriously ill, or needs an operation? With Earth no bigger than a bright star, the crew will be on their own.

They will have a ship's doctor, just like those aboard some ships that sail on Earth's oceans. In addition, all the crew will get basic medical training, so that if the doctor falls ill, they won't be entirely without skills.

Another key to medical health will be **telemedicine**.

Telemedicine is long-range radio and video assistance from doctors back on Earth.

For really serious illnesses, the Mars ship will carry advanced medical equipment, including a robotic surgeon, developed from those being used today, such as the da Vinci robot shown at right.

The machinery and surgical equipment onboard will have to be lightweight, compact, use little energy, and above all, be reliable for years at a time.

Marsnauts will also train for living on Mars after they have landed. Simulation chambers on Earth, which reproduce a human-made shelter in the Martian environment, will be used for planning and solving problems that may occur for the Marsnauts on Mars.

◄ Basketball-sized robots will patrol the ship in flight, checking on air quality and the crew's health.

◄ The European Space Agency (ESA), has plans for a set of living modules to test conditions for future Marsnauts. The modules will be in a laboratory, but the crew inside them will be sealed off from the outside world, just as they would be on Mars.

Dangerous journey

One of the biggest dangers facing astronauts on long space flights is that their muscles and bones gradually become weak and fragile.

▲ The Sun gives us heat and light, but also pours out **radiation**.

On short space flights, astronauts often feel sick for a while until they get used to the **weightless** feeling of free fall. Anti-sickness pills are helpful and the sickness usually passes in a short while.

On longer trips, the weightless environment leads to much more serious problems. Muscles have so little work to do that they go slack, making regular workouts on exercise machines vital.

An astronaut exercising on a treadmill

Astronauts floating freely in a space station module

▲ Astronauts use treadmills as well as other exercise equipment to stay fit in the International Space Station.

Another problem is that here on Earth, human bodies make new bone cells and get rid of old ones. In the weightless conditions of space, this continuous replacement process slows down considerably, leaving bones weak and brittle.

One solution would be to have a part of the Mars ship rotate, giving the Marsnauts inside a sensation of **gravity**. Daily sessions would keep the bone replacement process in working order.

► This huge Mars ship is one of the most advanced designs that could be built with the technology available today. Power to leave Earth's orbit would come from a nuclear motor, and rotating sections would provide a sense of weight, so the crew could stay healthy.

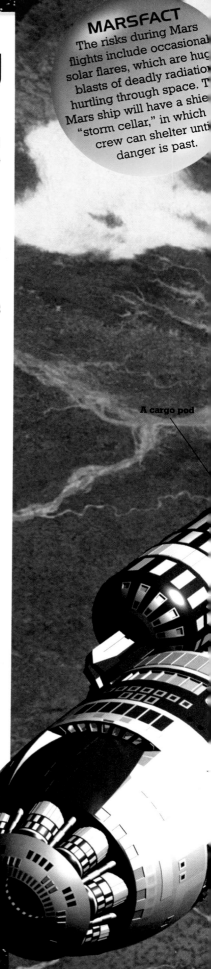

A cargo pod

MARSFACT
The risks during Mars flights include occasional solar flares, which are huge blasts of deadly radiation hurtling through space. The Mars ship will have a shielded "storm cellar," in which crew can shelter until danger is past.

A rotating crew section

A radio antenna

Fuel tanks for the main engines

Solar panels will provide electricity

A rotating crew section

Mars lander module

The command module

A Marsnaut to scale

Forces of gravity

Gravity varies on different planets, depending on their size and makeup. A person weighing 140 pounds (64 kilograms) on Earth would weigh just 23.3 pounds (10.7 kilograms) on the Moon, which is much smaller. Explorers on Mars will be about one-third of their weight back on Earth.

To keep astronauts healthy on the long flight to Mars, a ship similar to the one shown here may be needed. The design includes two sections that rotate around a main body. People inside each spinning section would have a feeling of weight, which would be just enough to keep their bodies in good shape.

We do not know yet whether the one-third gravity of Mars is strong enough to keep the bones and muscles of Marsnauts healthy on long stays. More research is needed before that question can be answered for sure.

First humans on Mars

After the Mars ship has successfully reached Mars orbit, the next step will be landing safely on the surface. The landing craft will have a **heat shield**, parachutes, and braking rockets to slow it down.

Getting ready for landing will be a busy time for the crew. When all systems have been checked as "go," bolts will unlatch to allow the lander to pull away from the mother, or main, ship. Next, the lander will rotate to face in the right direction. Then the rockets will roar into action for a minute or so, to nudge the lander out of orbit. Next stop, Mars!

◀ This living module design is an inflatable two-floor plastic and steel tube that can be erected quickly and easily.

▲ Future Marsnauts pose for the camera after landing on the red planet.

Strong cables keep the living module steady in sandstorms

Flight through the thin Martian atmosphere will not be smooth. The lander will shake and shudder as it hurtles down. The heat shield will glow cherry-red as it protects the craft from the heat of passing gas particles. When the lander's speed has slowed enough, a set of huge parachutes will pop open to slow the lander even more, getting it ready for landing.

▶ A future six-wheeled Mars rover rolls down a lightweight ramp.

The lander will hover on its braking rockets a few feet above the ground, then slowly come down to a soft landing. When the rockets shut off, there will be quiet, except for the creaking sounds of cooling metal. The Marsnauts will probably breathe sighs of relief, once they have landed safely!

A look through the lander's ports will show a rocky landscape, lit by the small Sun glowing through a pinkish sky. For the Marsnauts, there will be a whole new world out there, just waiting to be explored . . .

The gentle light of Mars

Human eyes work better than the finest camera lens because they can compensate well for varying light levels. For example, light that is ten times dimmer seems only about half as bright to the human eye.

Mars is farther away from the Sun than Earth is, so the sunlight reaching it is weaker, just 25 percent as strong as on our planet. Thanks to our eyes' way of seeing, daylight on Mars will seem to be about 80 percent of Earth's daylight levels – similar to the difference between daylight in the afternoon compared to daylight at noon.

The landscape will probably remind the Marsnauts of Earth's deserts. The sky will have a pale salmon-pink shade, instead of the dazzling blue of home.

▲ Marsnauts load up research equipment for a survey trip.

MARSFACT
Mars flights will be risky and expensive, so why bother to go? Why not stay at home? These were the same questions people asked when humans first started visiting space. The quest for new horizons is something that is part of being a human.

Dome dwellers

On Mars, humans will have to stay in sealed, air-filled bases. This is because there is not enough oxygen for them to breathe.

Dome homes will give Marsnauts room to work and relax. The domes will provide air, warmth, and comfort. A summer's day on Mars can be as mild as 68°Fahrenheit (20°Celsius) in warmer regions – but the nights are *extremely* cold. With no thick blanket of atmosphere like Earth's to hold the heat in, midnight on Mars reaches an ultra-chilly -220°Fahrenheit (-140°Celsius)!

▲ The Mars Society is a group dedicated to making flights to Mars possible. The society sets up domes in harsh climates to test people and equipment for a mission to Mars.

▲ Biosphere 2 in Arizona, U.S.A., was built to see whether people and crops could thrive in a sealed environment. Some of the test staff who lived there found life difficult, but experiments with growing crops still continue.

▶ A possible future dome on Mars. Fresh fruit and vegetables will make good eating for the crew of a future Mars base.

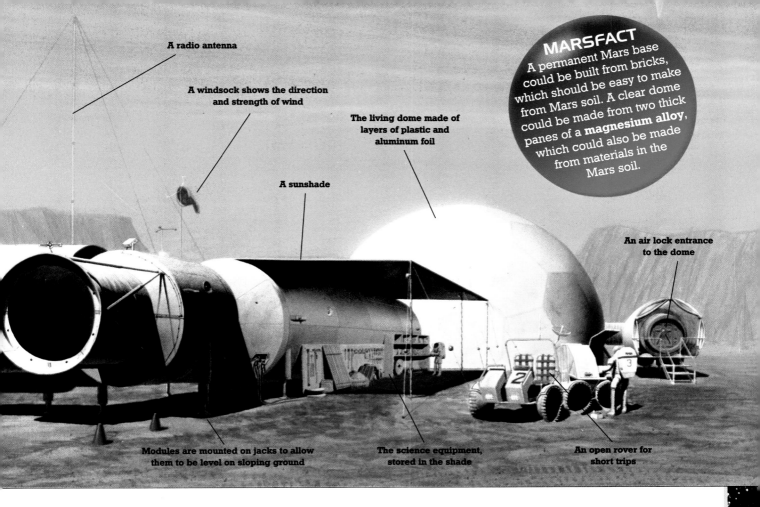

A radio antenna

A windsock shows the direction and strength of wind

The living dome made of layers of plastic and aluminum foil

A sunshade

An air lock entrance to the dome

Modules are mounted on jacks to allow them to be level on sloping ground

The science equipment, stored in the shade

An open rover for short trips

F or the first missions to Mars, domes will probably be simple and small, little more than survival systems for short stays. Later Marsnauts may need long-term accommodation. One idea is to bury domes under layers of soil. This would keep the heat in at night, and in daytime give protection from the Sun's rays, because the thin Martian atmosphere screens out very little solar radiation.

▲ The tube shaped sections of this future Mars base are parts of the cargo ships that would have brought supplies from Earth.

▼ An ESA (European Space Agency) idea for a science base, made from clip-together modules.

Robots go first, humans go later

Robert Zubrin is the founder of the Mars Society. An aerospace engineer and a writer, Zubrin believes that going to Mars will be very different from 1960s and 1970s Apollo missions to the Moon. Once on the surface of the Moon, astronauts had only a short time to explore, as their supplies were limited by what they could carry in their two-man landing module.

Zubrin's plan is for uncrewed Mars landers to reach Mars long before any humans go there. Robotic machinery on the landers would create a big storehouse of fuel, water, and oxygen from the Martian atmosphere and soil.

More uncrewed landers would take the components of a base. Zubrin's idea means that a crewed ship need carry far fewer supplies, cutting costs dramatically. It also means that when humans finally land on Mars, they will have a comfy, ready-made base to live in, with the supplies they need already stockpiled and ready for use.

▲ This is a design for a robot plane that could fly on mapping missions through the very thin Martian atmosphere.

Rovers and flyers

Traveling across Mars will mean a new generation of machines for transport. They will be specially designed for the cold and dusty environment.

Mars' land area is as big as the Earth's, so future Marsnauts will have no shortage of places to visit. Trips beyond walking range from a base will require survival equipment for the crew. Explorers will always have to wear suits with an air supply, and will need overnight protection from the cold.

◄▼ These pictures show how a Mars plane could arrive in a protective cone (1), parachute to lower altitudes (2), unfold in mid-air (3, 4), level out safely (5), and then switch on its engine to fly over the surface (6).

Mars planes will have long, thin wings to supply enough **lift** in the thin air. Jet engines will not work in the largely carbon dioxide atmosphere, so power could come from a small, liquid-fueled rocket engine.

On the ground, rovers will come in two types: an open Short Distance Rover (SDR) for local trips, and a sealed "mobile home" Long Distance Rover (LDR), for exploring farther away.

▼ Long trips will be carried out in big LDRs, giving Marsnauts a comfortable environment.

▶ Marsnauts have to stay in their suits when using an SDR. Each wheel is driven by a powerful electric motor in its hub.

The LDR will be a combined mobile home and fully equipped science laboratory. It will have heat, light, and air, so crews can take off their suits and relax. A microwave oven will be used to heat up ready-made meals, and to cook fresh vegetables grown in the base's greenhouse unit, from seeds brought from Earth.

 ## A very slow conversation

The distance between Earth and Mars varies continually as the planets move around the Sun, but it is never less than 35 million miles (56 million km).

The distance may create a few problems for Marsnauts when they talk to mission control on Earth.

Even though radio signals travel at the speed of light, 186,000 miles/sec (300,000 km/sec), a signal still takes more than three minutes to make a one-way journey. With nearly seven minutes to wait for a reply, Marsnauts won't want to talk about anything too urgent!

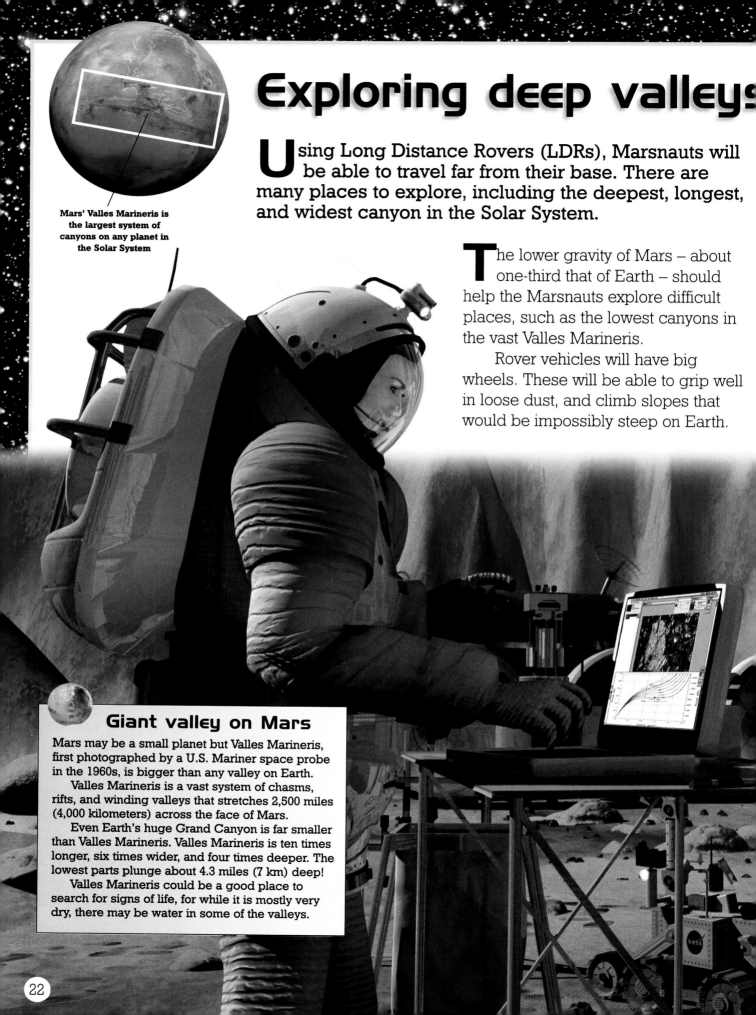

Exploring deep valleys

Mars' Valles Marineris is the largest system of canyons on any planet in the Solar System

Using Long Distance Rovers (LDRs), Marsnauts will be able to travel far from their base. There are many places to explore, including the deepest, longest, and widest canyon in the Solar System.

The lower gravity of Mars – about one-third that of Earth – should help the Marsnauts explore difficult places, such as the lowest canyons in the vast Valles Marineris.

Rover vehicles will have big wheels. These will be able to grip well in loose dust, and climb slopes that would be impossibly steep on Earth.

Giant valley on Mars

Mars may be a small planet but Valles Marineris, first photographed by a U.S. Mariner space probe in the 1960s, is bigger than any valley on Earth.

Valles Marineris is a vast system of chasms, rifts, and winding valleys that stretches 2,500 miles (4,000 kilometers) across the face of Mars.

Even Earth's huge Grand Canyon is far smaller than Valles Marineris. Valles Marineris is ten times longer, six times wider, and four times deeper. The lowest parts plunge about 4.3 miles (7 km) deep!

Valles Marineris could be a good place to search for signs of life, for while it is mostly very dry, there may be water in some of the valleys.

◄ Climbing experience could be useful for Marsnauts when they have to explore hard to reach places.

The radio will be used for voice and data communications

Dust could make working difficult. Only careful wiping will keep faceplates clean

Explorers hope to find signs of life in Valles Marineris. Some scientists think that if there is anything alive on Mars it will be down there, where there is some protection from the worst of the harsh climate.

Another possibility is that there may be cave systems on the sides of the valleys. These may also contain signs of life or even have underground springs. If so, the Valles could become a new home for Marsnauts, with a safe sheltered base, made by sealing off the entrance of a cave with an air lock.

◄ Future Marsnauts use a laptop computer to record information as they explore a valley bottom. A small wheeled robot can be used in places that are too awkward for humans to reach.

MARSFACT
Dust storms on Mars blow at 100 miles an hour (160 km/h) or more. These storms wear away exposed surfaces, and could clog delicate machinery. Protective coatings and filters on equipment will be needed to repel the dust.

Green Mars?

One day it may be possible to make Mars a more comfortable place for humans to live.

▲ The water frozen into the Martian **ice caps** is enough to make a sea about 300 feet (100 m) deep.

If missions to Mars become common, then domed bases will grow to accommodate the demands of new visitors. Cave bases could be expanded when needed, by drilling into the rock. Perhaps some Marsnauts will decide to stay permanently on the red planet, even raising families there. If so, their children will become the first real "Martians." To them it will be home.

► Trees grow inside a future community on Mars. Trees supply oxygen to breathe.

MARSFACT
Many novels have been written about colonizing the red planet. One of the first was *The Sands of Mars*, written by Arthur C. Clarke in 1951. Kim Stanley Robinson's *Red Mars* of 1992 is the first of three novels that cover the subject in great detail.

▼ Future Marsnauts look on as a train carries ice from the polar regions. When melted, the ice could provide water for people at a Mars base.

In the distant future, it may be possible to turn Mars into a smaller twin of Earth. Mars has water, even if most of it is frozen at the poles. If the ice was melted, there would be enough to cover much of Mars with a shallow sea. Special breeds of hardy plants could steadily add oxygen to the atmosphere until, one day, a human might be able to survive on the surface without the protection of a space suit.

Trees grow in a park-like "green" zone

Solar panels on the roof provide electricity

Living and working levels are below the green zone

Watery worldlets in space

There are lots of ideas for making Mars more Earthlike, but many of them may not be possible.

One of these far-out ideas is to guide a comet made of ice toward Mars. Millions of these dirty snowballs drift through space. The comet would graze the upper atmosphere of Mars, and the heat of this high-speed entry would spray steam and water across the planet.

One estimate is that a comet "snowball" just 6.2 miles (10 kilometers) across could provide enough water for a Mars-wide sea about 6.5 feet (2 meters) deep.

It is a great idea, though full of danger. Is it likely ever to happen? Only time will tell . . .

The comet head is too small to be visible here. The tail is made of gas and dust, vaporized by the Sun's heat

Exploring the frozen surface of a comet

Beyond Mars

After Mars, what next? There will be other planets to visit, as well as many moons and **asteroid** space rocks. Even farther away, the stars await . . .

Mars has two moons, called Phobos and Deimos. These moons are lumps of rock only a few miles across. Other moons will make more interesting targets for exploration. Jupiter's moon, Europa, is thought to have a huge ocean, locked under a thick layer of ice. Is there life in the dark waters? One day humans might go there to find out for sure.

▲ This sci-fi vision from the 1950s shows a hollowed-out asteroid converted to a space habitat.

Hayabusa space probe on the asteroid Itokawa

◀ The Hayabusa uncrewed space probe landed on an asteroid in 2005.

▲ Future Marsnauts inspect the rocky moon of Deimos (1), and the icy surface of Europa (2), one of the moons of Jupiter.

Asteroids consist of millions of space rocks, ranging from tiny boulders to Ceres, a dwarf planet 620 miles (1,000 kilometers) across. One day asteroids could be mined for their mineral wealth. Even today, space rocks are used for this. One of the world's biggest nickel mines, at Sudbury, in Canada, is actually the remains of a comet that collided with Earth millions of years ago.

Does sci-fi point a way to the stars?

Many sci-fi stories feature spacecraft that can zip across the Universe in no time at all. For many writers, getting fictional characters around quickly is an essential part of telling a fast-paced story. But sci-fi reflects an important point – space is vast, and rockets are not fast enough to take humans much farther than Mars, unless they are willing to spend most, or all, of their lives sitting inside a spaceship.

Weirdly, sci-fi may come true one day. At least one researcher thinks that it may be possible to "stretch" and "shrink" the fabric of space itself, using some form of distortion device. The spacecraft may move slowly or perhaps not move at all – instead the distorter stretches space behind it and shrinks space in front. Result? A journey across the Universe in next to no time!

Traveling to planets beyond Mars involves long journeys that last for many years. To cut flight times for astronauts, nuclear engines are one possibility. Another is the **ion-drive** – instead of a huge roar of flame, an ion-drive emits an electric glow, with a small thrust that keeps firing continuously. Eventually this leads to much higher speeds than even the most powerful rocket engine.

▼ An ion-drive spacecraft moves into orbit near Jupiter, some time in the future. Crew modules are in the nose section. Craft like this may be developed from the ion-drives (arrowed, bottom left) used today.

Timeline

Here are discoveries and achievements marking the long and difficult future journey to Mars.

▲ Giovanni Schiaparelli, observer of *"canali"* on Mars.

▲ A Martian based the ones in the nove by H.G.Wells.

About 1500 B.C. The Ancient Egyptians observe the movement of Mars in the sky.

About 700 B.C. Mars, god of war, is one of the early Romans' three chief gods.

About 350 B.C. Greek philosopher Aristotle notes that Mars appears to be farther away than the Moon.

1580-1600 A.D. Danish astronomer Tycho Brahe measures the movement of Mars in the sky, over a number of years.

1609 Italian astronomer Galileo Galilei looks at Mars through his newly invented telescope.

1636-38 Another Italian astronomer, Francisco Fontana, makes the first known drawings of Mars.

1659 Dutch astronomer Christiaan Huygens sees Syrtis Major, a Martian feature that seems to change color with the seasons. He also calculates the size of Mars and the length of its day.

1666 French astronomer Giovanni Cassini observes one of the ice caps of Mars, and later measures its distance from Earth.

1698 Christiaan Huygens publishes his book *Cosmotheoros*, which discusses the possibility of life on other planets.

1781 British astronomer William Herschel concludes that the white areas around the poles of Mars are polar ice caps, similar to those on Earth.

1877 Italian astronomer Giovanni Schiaparelli produces a map of Mars, with channels ("*canali*") marked on it. He also labels several geographical features still known by the same names today.

1877 U.S. astronomer Asaph Hall discovers the two moons of Mars, Phobos and Deimos. The names mean "fear" and "dread," after the sons of Ares, the Greek god of war.

1895 U.S. astronomer Percival Lowell publishes *Mars*, the first of three books in which he writes about possible Martians living on the red planet. Lowell's theory is that they have built a vast canal system to take water from the poles to desert area

1898 British author H.G. Wells publishes *The Wa of the Worlds*. It inspires many other authors to write "Invasion of Earth" stories, as well as radio plays, TV series, a musical, and several movies.

1912 Swedish chemist Svante Arrhenius sugges that color changes seen on the face of Mars are caused by seasonal melting of the ice caps.

1920s First calculations estimate that temperatures on Mars probably reach no more tha 60°F (15°C) in daytime and -120°F (-85°C) at nigh

1950 Most experts are still not sure whether the really are canals or not. U.S. astronomer Clyde Tombaugh suggests that they are fractures in the surface, created by the impact of giant meteors.

▼ Many people have tried to show what a race of Martians might look like. This tall Martian has hug lungs to breathe the thin air. It was created by arti Frank R. Paul, for a 1939 issue of the popular sci-fi magazine *Fantastic Adventures*.

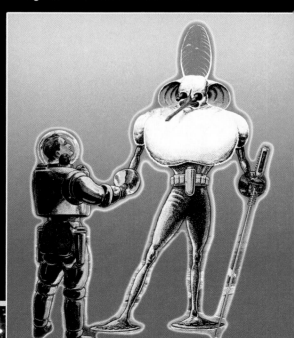

1953 The International Mars Committee is formed to observe Mars during its close approach of 1954.

1964 The first successful flight past Mars is made by a space probe. The U.S. Mariner 4 took 22 pictures while passing 6,117 miles (9,845 kilometers) above the planet's surface. Mariner 4 also measured the very low air pressure, more than 100 times thinner than at ground level on Earth.

1973 Several Russian space probes make partially successful Mars approaches.

1976 The U.S. Viking 1 and Viking 2 space probes land on Mars, test the air and soil, and return information for several years. Altogether, the two landers take more than 50,000 pictures.

1996 The Mars Pathfinder mission lands the first Mars rover, a 23-pound (10.6-kg) wheeled robot, called *Sojourner*. The microwave-sized machine works extremely well, but contact with it is lost after 83 sols (Martian days).

2001 Mars Odyssey orbits the red planet, using its instruments to hunt for evidence of water and volcano eruptions.

2004 Mars Exploration Rover (MER) missions land two rovers on Mars. The rovers, named *Spirit* and *Opportunity*, are designed to last for about 90 sols, but remain in working order after more than two years on the surface.

2004 Long-term human space flight aims are announced for the U.S. NASA space agency. They include plans to return to the Moon as early as the year 2015. Human flights to Mars, building on experience gained on the Moon, could start sometime after 2020-25.

2006 Getting safely to Mars is very difficult – and the high failure rate of spacecraft traveling there proves it. By 2006, 37 missions had left Earth for the red planet, and only 18 were successful. Others were victims of various problems along the way. It's something that has been labelled the "Mars Curse."

► A future Mars base, conceived as a joint U.S.-European venture. It has two decks, with an air lock door extending underneath. This design could be home for up to six Marsnauts staying on the surface for several weeks.

◄ How the Martian polar regions might look when gas geysers blow through the icy surface.

2006 Mars Reconnaissance Orbiter (MRO) is a multi-purpose spacecraft designed to explore Mars from orbit. It uses **aerobraking** to achieve a close orbit, by flying through the incredibly thin upper atmosphere to slow down gradually.

2008 The Phoenix Mars Lander will explore the Martian polar regions and drill through the ice to see if there is any life underneath.

2015 Planning for a human Mars mission may be at a detailed stage.

2020 Human Mars flights could be in final preparation.

2025 The first Mars base could be set up, opening the way for Mars colonies and humans living on a new world.

◄ This picture of a hilly landscape feature, taken by a Viking space probe in 1976, was declared by some so-called experts as evidence of a skilled race of Martians, who carved a giant "face" in the rock. A later space probe, with better cameras, showed the facial appearance was just a trick of the light.

Glossary

Here are explanations of many of the technical terms used in this book.

▲ This Mars spacecraft has a large dish antenna (arrowed) used to send information back to Earth.

Aerobraking A way of slowing down by swooping through the ultra-thin upper atmosphere of a planet.

Alien Anything from "out there." In sci-fi stories, the word is used for creatures from other planets, often a danger to humans.

Antarctica Frozen continent around the South Pole on Earth.

Antenna A rod or dish-shaped aerial that transmits or receives radio and TV signals.

Asteroid A lump of space rock, one of millions that never formed a planet. Asteroids range from boulder-sized to nearly as large as a dwarf planet.

Atmosphere The blanket of gases that surrounds many planets. Earth's air is a mixture of mostly nitrogen and oxygen. Mars has a very thin atmosphere that is mostly carbon dioxide gas.

Carbon dioxide The gas composing most of the Martian atmosphere. On Earth, humans and other animals inhale oxygen, and exhale carbon dioxide as a waste gas.

Comet Often called "dirty snowballs" in space, comets are usually a frozen mixture of ice, dust, and rock. When far away from the Sun, a comet is dark and cold. Nearer to the Sun, heat vaporizes some of the ice, creating a tail of glowing gas and dust.

Dwarf planet One of the smaller planets that orbit the Sun, such as Pluto and Eris.

Gravity The force of attraction between objects. Massive objects have a stronger gravitational pull than smaller ones. The state of having almost no gravity at all is called microgravity or weightlessness.

Heat shield An outer shell designed to protect a delicate lander spacecraft during its entry through the upper atmosphere.

Hubble Space Telescope A powerful telescope in orbit around the Earth, where it can view space without its pictures being spoiled by dust in the Earth's atmosphere.

Hydrogen A colorless, odorless gas that exists naturally in the Universe.

Ice cap Area around the poles of a planet where ice forms. Earth and Mars both have ice caps. Ice caps on Earth are frozen water, on Mars they are made mostly of frozen carbon dioxide with some frozen water.

Ion-drive An engine that uses a beam of electrically charged particles, instead of an exhaust flame, for propulsion.

Lander A spacecraft built to make contact with the surface of a space object. A "hard" lander is made to crash into the ground, a "soft" lander takes down an instrument package or other load gently.

Lift The upward force acting on an aircraft caused by movement of air around the wing.

Liquid fuel A fuel system for rockets, typically super cold liquid hydrogen, which is burned when mixed with liquid oxygen.

Magnesium alloy A mix of magnesium, a silvery white metal, with another metal.

Module A section of a spacecraft. Examples are crew, cargo, or communications modules.

Moon A smaller companion that orbits around a planet. Earth's Moon is a sphere 2,160 miles (3,476 km) across. Mars' two potato-shaped moons, Phobos and Deimos, are tiny – even the bigger Phobos is just 13.7 miles (22 km) across.

Nuclear motor A power system that uses energy from colliding atoms to create heat. This is used to create a super hot rocket exhaust that creates more power than liquid fuel systems.

Orbit The curving path one space object takes around another. The Earth orbits the Sun once a year; the Moon orbits the Earth every 27.3 days. Mars is farther from the Sun, so has a larger orbit, with a year that is double the length of the Earth's.

Planet A large body in space that orbits the Sun, or another star. The Solar System has four small rocky planets and four gas giants.

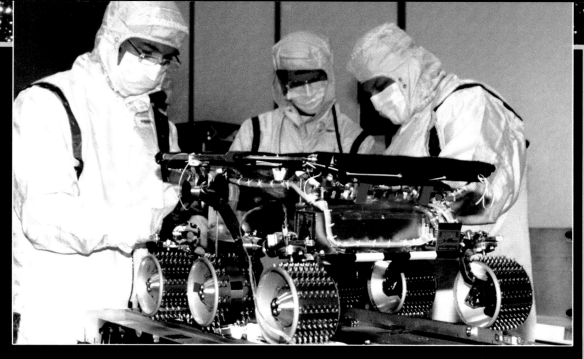

► Technicians prepare the *Sojourner* robot rover, which landed on Mars in July 1997. During its mission the rover sent 550 pictures back to Earth, and studied Martian rocks, soil, wind, and weather.

Radiation The range of wave energy found in nature. Visible light is one example, as are invisible infra-red heat rays. High-energy radiation from the Sun, such as ultra-violet rays, can cause immense damage to living cells.

Rift valley A huge valley formed by a crack in the Earth's crust, or outer rocky layer.

Rover A vehicle that moves on another planet, driven by humans or guided by computer systems.

Sol A Martian day, which lasts for 24 hours 37.5 minutes. "Sol" is also another name for the Sun.

Solar panel A device made of silicon that converts the energy in light into electricity.

Solar System The Sun, together with the planets, dwarf planets, moons, comets, asteroids, rocks, and dust that circle it.

Telemedicine Medical treatment that is carried out at a distance, using radio, TV, or the Internet, to link a patient with a doctor. The da Vinci robot surgeon can be directed by a surgeon thousands of kilometers away.

Weightlessness Also called "free fall," it happens when floating in space, where there is no strong gravity field pulling in one direction. The Earth exerts a one-gravity (1G) force at its surface. Mars is a smaller planet with gravity about one-third as strong.

Year The time it takes for a planet to complete a full orbit around the Sun. A day is the time that a planet takes to rotate once around its own axis.

▲ Space walks are a regular part of an astronaut's flight duties.

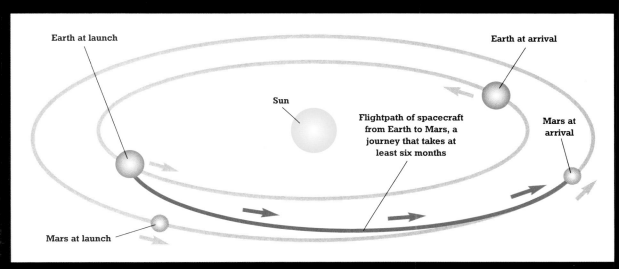

Earth at launch

Earth at arrival

Sun

Flightpath of spacecraft from Earth to Mars, a journey that takes at least six months

Mars at arrival

Mars at launch

◄ Nothing travels in a straight line in space. The red line at left shows the curving course a spacecraft takes when going from Earth to Mars.

Index

aerobraking 29, 30
alien 8, 9, 30
antenna 15, 19, 30
Apollo program 5, 19
asteroid 26, 30

Biosphere 2 18
books, magazines, movies
    Cosmotheoros 28
    Fantastic Adventures 28
    Mars 28
    Red Mars 24
    The Sands of Mars 24
    The War of the Worlds 8,
      9, 28

carbon dioxide 9, 21, 30
Ceres 26
comets 25, 26, 30

da Vinci robot surgeon 13, 31

gravity 14, 15, 22, 30, 31

health 13, 14, 15
heat shield 16, 30

International Mars Committee
    29
ion-drive 27, 30

Jupiter 5, 26, 27

liquid fuel 11, 21, 30

Mars
    atmosphere 7, 18, 19, 20,
      21, 24, 30
    bases 18, 19, 24, 29
    canals 5, 28
    deserts 5, 7, 12, 28
    distance from Earth 5, 21,
      28
    dust 23
    god of war 4, 28

gravity 14, 15, 22, 30
ice caps, poles 5, 7, 9, 24,
    28, 29, 30
life, Martians 5, 8, 9, 22,
    23, 24, 28, 29
light 17
Marsnauts 12, 13, 16, 17,
    18, 19, 20, 21, 22, 23, 24,
    29
Olympus Mons 6, 7
rocks 8, 9
rust 7
seas 7, 24, 25
ship 10, 11
Society 18, 19
sol (day) 7, 29, 31
Syrtis Major 28
temperature 7, 18, 28
Valles Marineris 7, 22, 23
mining 26
module 10, 13, 15, 16, 19, 27,
    30
Moon, moons 2, 5, 7, 19, 29,
    30

nuclear motor 11, 14, 27, 30

orbit 4, 10, 14, 16, 29, 30

people
    Antoniadi, Eugène 5
    Aristotle 28
    Arrhenius, Svante 28
    Brahe, Tycho 28
    Burroughs, Edgar Rice 9
    Cassini, Giovanni 28
    Clarke, Arthur C. 24
    Fontana, Francisco 28
    Galilei, Galileo 28
    Hall, Asaph 28
    Herschel, William 28
    Huygens, Christiaan 28
    Lowell, Percival 5, 8, 28
    Paul, Frank R. 28
    Robinson, Kim Stanley 24

Schiaparelli, Giovanni 5,
    28
Spielberg, Steven 9
Tombaugh, Clyde 28
Wells, H.G. 8, 9, 28
Zubrin, Robert 19
Phobos, Deimos 7, 26, 28, 30
places
    Antarctica 8, 30
    Grand Canyon 22
    Mount Everest 6
    Sudbury 26
planets, dwarf planets 4, 5,
    26, 31

radiation 14, 19, 31

simulation chamber 13
solar flares 14
solar panels 15, 25, 31
Solar System 4, 31
space agencies
    ESA 13, 19
    NASA 29
spacecraft, probes, rovers
    Hayabusa 26
    Hubble Space Telescope
      6, 30
    International Space Station
      14
    lander 16, 17, 19, 30
    LDR rover 21, 22
    Mariner 5, 22, 29
    Mars plane 20, 21
    MER 29
    MRO 29
    Odyssey 29
    Opportunity 29
    Pathfinder 29
    Phoenix lander 9, 29
    Russian 29
    SDR rover 21
    Sojourner 29, 31
    Space Shuttle 11
    Spirit 7, 29

Viking 6, 29
space distorter 27
space suits 12, 20, 21, 24
Sun 4, 14, 17, 19

telemedicine 13, 31

weightless 14, 31

year 4

Acknowledgements
We wish to thank all those people
who have helped to create this
publication. Information and images
were supplied by:
Individuals:
Mat Irvine
David Jefferis
Rory McLeish
iStockphoto:
    Robert Buss
    Kan Kaliciak
    Robert Skold
NASA Sources:
    Mark Dowman
    John Frassanito & Associates
    Ron Miller
    Pat Rawlings
Organizations:
    Alpha Archive
    Amblin Entertainment
    Arizona State University
    Dreamworks Pictures
    ESA European Space Agency
    Intuitive Surgical, Inc.
    JPL Jet Propulsion Laboratory
    Lowell Observatory
    NASA Space Agency
    NASDA, JAXA, Japanese Space
      Agencies
    Paramount Pictures
    The Mars Society
Edgar Rice Burroughs novels
published by Del Rey Books.

Printed in the U.S.A.